MW00794919

A LITTLE BOOK OF
ROSES

A Little Book of Roses

Nancy Arnott

ARIEL BOOKS

**Andrews McMeel
Publishing**

Kansas City

www.andrewsmcmeel.com

ISBN: 0-8362-5217-9
Library of Congress Catalog Card Number: 97-74512

CONTENTS

INTRODUCTION

"Red Rose, proud Rose, sad Rose of all my days!" wrote the great Irish bard, William Butler Yeats, and he spoke for poets everywhere. No other flower has captured the human imagination as the rose has. Its rare beauty and transporting scent stirs not only the souls of writers, but also of sweethearts, who trade long-stemmed blooms as tokens of their regard; gardeners, who toil all year long to be rewarded each June with a little glimpse—and smell— of heaven; and everyone who appreciates natural beauty. Some may claim another blossom as their favorite, but few can resist the lure of the rose. Year after year, it reigns as the queen of flowers.

ROSE
OF THE
AGES

Could rose gardens possibly have grown alongside the great pyramids? The historical roots of the rose can be traced all the way back to antiquity, and evidence of rose cultivation has been found in Egypt at least since the fourth century B.C.

Through the ages, 150 different species have been developed by enthusiasts around the globe. They all belong to the botanical genus *Rosa*, which is part of the family known as Rosaceae. Some of the rose's familiar relations in this large and diverse grouping are the apple, the cherry, the strawberry, and even the almond.

The rose grows throughout the Northern Hemisphere, from China to the Americas; and although it is the official flower of the United States as a whole and of Iowa, New York, North Dakota, and the District of Columbia in particular, it originated in the Old World. Most wild roses (which are also known as species roses to distinguish them from

hybrids), were first found growing in Asia, and came to America by way of Europe. The celebrated French rose, or *Rosa gallica,* was first found growing wild in France.

Even though species roses are still prized and popular, most roses grown today are hybrids. Hybrids are produced by crossbreeding two existing species, whether they are wild or hybrids themselves, which enables breeders to create new roses

that combine the best
qualities of their par-
ents. One of the first
such sensations in the
rose-growing world was
the hybrid perpetual, in-
troduced in the 1860s.
Hybrid perpetuals put
out large, lush blossoms
in white, pink, or red,
but the secret of the
plant's success with gar-

deners was its hardiness; it proved unusually resistant to cold temperatures.

As sturdy as the hybrid perpetual was, and as lovely as its flowers were, it did not bloom profusely enough to satisfy enthusiasts. Another gardeners' favorite, the tea rose (*Rosa odorata*), produced more lavish flowers and enjoyed a long blooming season. It grew on a two-foot-tall bush that freely yielded

clusters of white, pink, or yellow blooms. Its striking, spicy scent, which suggested its nickname, provided an added attraction. Tea roses were originally brought to Europe from China.

Enterprising hybridizers who wanted the best of both worlds arrived at a solution: crossing the hybrid perpetual with the tea rose. Bred together, these two varieties produced the hybrid tea. It is a freely

blooming plant with a more ele-
gantly tapered silhouette than its
many-petaled ancestors. Its flowers
are characterized by high, pointed
centers, on which they are judged in
horticultural competitions. The hybrid tea is the most popular rose
species in the world today. It is a
Valentine's Day best-
seller at every
florist's shop;
one dozen long-

stemmed roses invariably consists of twelve perfect hybrid tea blooms.

CHILDREN OF THE HYBRID TEA

The hybrid tea is what most of us mentally see and smell when we hear the word "rose," but it is not the only variety enjoyed and grown by modern rosarians. (This term was coined in 1864 to describe cultivators of roses.) Most of the following varieties can claim the hybrid tea as one of its parents:

Polyantha: This low-growing bush, whose name in Greek means "many flowered," resulted from a cross between the hybrid tea and the species rose *Rosa multiflora*. It produces abundant clusters of small flowers from late spring through early fall.

Floribunda: An offspring of the polyantha and the hybrid tea, this

bush, too, has a long blooming season. Its slightly larger flowers look more like hybrid tea blooms, and the bush grows no more than five feet tall.

Grandiflora: As its name suggests, this cross between the floribunda and the hybrid tea grows tall—sometimes more than six feet—but its blooms form a happy medium between those of its parents.

Miniature roses: These compact

plants, descended from a species rose called *Rosa chinensis minima*, are tiny in both bush and bloom.

Bushes range from six inches to four feet in height, blooms from a quarter inch (the size of a pea) to two inches (the size of a lime) in diameter. The smallest of these plants are called micro minis.

English roses, also known as *David Austin roses:* The nostalgia for the pre–hybrid tea roses that grew in great-grandmother's garden prompted English hybridizer David

Austin to develop roses combining
the large, cabbagelike form of older
varieties with the hardiness and dis-
ease resistance of modern roses.
These are proving to be very popular with adventurous American
gardeners who are looking to branch
out from the hybrid tea.

REASONS TO LOVE ROSES

One of the main reasons that roses are so beloved is their distinctive perfume. Another is their variety of colors, which run the gamut from the delicate to the bold.

Scent is the main attraction in some roses, a second feature in others, but all roses possess a fragrance

of one degree or another, from the vaguely floral to the intoxicatingly spiced. Old-fashioned damask roses are famous for their heady perfume, and many modern hybrid teas were bred to produce blooms with particularly strong scents.

Attar of roses, an oil distilled from rose flowers, has been prized since the ancient Persians began extracting it thousands of years ago as a basis for perfumes and cosmetics. This oil, drawn primarily from damask roses grown in Bulgaria, is still used in the modern fragrance industry—but *five thousand pounds* of fresh rose petals are needed to make one pound of attar! Flowers must also be harvested before sunrise, when their oil content is greatest. Now it is easy to see why fine perfumes made from it are so costly.

Rose oil is also used in *aromatherapy,* the art of using scent to

positively influence mood and health.
Aromatherapists believe that rose is
the fragrance of the heart. They
recommend its essence for relieving
depression and sadness, and restoring
balance between the emotions and
the body. They also consider it an
aphrodisiac, an opinion shared by
the more decadent citizens of the
late Roman Empire, who piled their
boudoirs high with rose petals to
create a sensual atmosphere.

The other great charm of roses is more varied than their scent. These flowers are cultivated today in just about every color of the rainbow, from the familiar red, pink, yellow, and white to apricot, copper, gold, and mauve. Bicolor and multicolor roses wear stripes or sport petals dominated by one color with contrasting edges or undersides. There are even "blue" and "black" roses, though the

blues are really bluish lavenders
and the blacks are rich, deep reds.

The color of a rose evolves
throughout the life cycle of the blossom, revealing itself as the bud
opens and fading as the bloom
wilts. Light intensity is also a factor.
Roses thrive in full sun and will not
reach their full potential without it.
But many days of intense summer
sun can ultimately bleach their
vibrant hues.

Color also plays a more fanciful role for rose lovers. Since Roman times, people have attributed meanings to certain flowers. This notion, which peaked in the Victorian era, allows the giver to express personal sentiments through his choice of flower, and the receiver to read meaning into every blossom. In the language of flowers, the meaning of roses varies—sometimes greatly—according to their color. *White* symbolizes purity or worthiness ("I am worthy of your love"); *red* symbolizes love; *yellow* symbolizes jealousy.

ROSES IN YOUR HOME

One of the joys of growing roses is bringing them in-doors to fill your home with their beauty and perfume. It's best to cut roses off their bushes in either the early morning or the late afternoon, avoiding the wilting heat of midday. Put each stem into a pail of lukewarm water as soon as it is cut.

Leave any buds that are closed tight; if you snip them at this stage, they will never open. Also avoid fully opened blooms, which won't last long in a vase before they start drooping and dropping their petals. The ideal stems to cut are those with partially opened buds or half-opened blooms.

Use well-sharpened pruning shears and cut the stems at a 45-degree angle, making a sharp cut with one motion. Cut each stem at a point just above a five-leaflet leaf; on most stems there should be several from which to choose. Making the cuts at these places will encourage new shoots to spring forth, renewing your supply of blooms to enjoy. Also, to avoid stunting a bush's growth, never cut more than a third of its stems in any cutting or pruning session.

Keep the cut blooms refrigerated in water until you are ready to arrange them in a vase. To groom them for arrangement, strip off any leaves and thorns that would be below the water in the vase or other container. If these are left on, they will rot, producing bacteria that will cause the stems to decay rapidly.

Holding the stem underwater (to

prevent stem damage), make a fresh, angled cut at the end of each stem. Place the flowers in the vase and add water up to about two-thirds the length of the stems. You might want to use a preservative powder from a local florist or garden shop. Crushed aspirin or a teaspoon of sugar or lemony soft drink have all been proposed as floral life extenders.

To keep enjoying the beauty of

your roses through the fall and win-
ter, however, you'll need to dry or
preserve them. Cut the roses early
in the day, when they are richest in
essential oils, and then preserve
them using one of the following
three methods.

The first takes a little more time
and effort than the others, but it
holds the color best. Line the bot-
tom of an airtight container with an
inch of silica gel (available at

florists' and garden stores); place
the flowers face-up in the gel in a
single layer and sprinkle more gel
over and between the petals, until

there is another inch of gel on top of the flowers; cover the container and allow the flowers to sit for three to four days, until they have dried completely.

The second method lets you preserve a whole bouquet at one time. Remove most of the leaves; gather the stems into a bunch, varying the flower heights; tie the stems together securely with a length of string; and hang the bunch upside down in a warm, dry place away from direct light until it is dried.

The third method is the simplest for drying petals and buds. Lay

them flat on a few layers of paper towels and stir or turn them over each day, until they are fully dried. For quicker results, lay the petals and buds in a single layer on a baking sheet and pop them into a cool oven (110 degrees), with the oven door slightly ajar to let the moisture escape. Shake the sheet occasionally to promote even drying. This process takes only an hour or two.

Fresh or dried, roses can be enjoyed in your home every day—and not just in flower arrangements. The following suggestions will start you thinking of creative ways to make your life a little "rosier."

Make a rose potpourri: Blend dried petals and/or buds of various

colors, using all roses or comple-
menting them with other blooms,
petals, and even spices. The ad-
dition of a fixative, such as pow-
dered orrisroot
or ground
gum ben-
zoin, will
give the
mixture
more
staying
power.

Try the following recipe for a floral-spice potpourri:

Ingredients:

$^1/_2$ pint rose buds

$^1/_2$ pint rose petals

1 ounce lavender

2 cinnamon sticks

strips of orange zest from 1 orange

1 ounce orrisroot powder

Lay the cinnamon sticks parallel or in an X shape in a container and arrange the other ingredients around

them. Optional: Add a few drops of rose essential oil to intensify or refresh the rose fragrance.

Add roses to your recipes: Petals from roses that have never been treated with chemicals are edible and can be used in their dried form to flavor foods. Fresh rose petals can be used to make jam. To create a beautiful sugared rose petal garnish for desserts, use a pastry brush to paint individual petals with a

thin film of beaten egg white. Coat
each petal with a light sprinkling of
granulated sugar and set on a plate
dusted with sugar until dry.

Use roses in your beauty regimen:
Rose water, a mild astringent, has
been used as a skin toner for cen-
turies. You can make your own by
adding ten drops of rose essential
oil to half a pint of vodka. Put the
mixture into a glass bottle and seal
it with a cork.

Take roses into the bathtub:
Make a relaxing and romantic rose
bath by adding several drops of rose
oil to a tub of warm water (do so

just before you step in so that the essential oil won't have time to evaporate) or by filling a small muslin bag with two ounces of dried rose petals and suspending it from the faucet so the water runs through it as the tub fills. Make your rose bath even more luxurious by scattering fresh petals over the water's surface. You can also concoct a rose foaming bath oil by adding a tablespoon each of rose oil